William Lowndes Yancey

Speeches of Willam L. Yancey, Senator from the State of Alabama

Made in the Senate of the Confederate States During the Session

Commencing on the 18th day of August, A.D. 1862

William Lowndes Yancey

Speeches of Willam L. Yancey, Senator from the State of Alabama
*Made in the Senate of the Confederate States During the Session Commencing on
the 18th day of August, A.D. 1862*

ISBN/EAN: 9783337155384

Printed in Europe, USA, Canada, Australia, Japan

Cover: Foto ©ninafisch / pixelio.de

More available books at **www.hansebooks.com**

OF

WILLIAM L. YANCEY, ESQ.,

SENATOR FROM

THE STATE OF ALABAMA;

Made in the Senate of the Confederate States,
During the Session Commencing on the 18th
day of August, A. D. 1862.

— -- ◄•► ——

ı

MONTGOMERY, ALA.:
MONTGOMERY ADVERTISER BOOK AND JOB OFFICE.

1862.

RETALIATION.

On the 21st of August, 1862, Mr. YANCEY introduced in the Senate the following

RESOLUTIONS

Expressing the sense of the Senate in respect to the violation of the laws and usages of civilized war by the Government of the United States.

I. *Resolved by the Senate of the Confederate States of America,* That the war which is now being waged by the United States, for the avowed purpose of subjugating the people of the several States of this Government to the dominion of the Government of the United States, is, in the opinion of the Senate, a war as well upon the people as upon the Government of the Confederate States of America; and that the principles upon which this Government and the governments of the several States which compose it, are founded, justify each citizen thereof, when the invading enemy enters upon the soil of his State, in taking up arms to defend his homestead and liberties, and in attacking the invader, either by individual action or in organized bands.

II. *Resolved,* That when any of our citizens shall exercise this sacred right, and shall by the fortune of war fall into the hands of the enemy, they are entitled to be treated as prisoners of war; and if they shall be treated otherwise, it is the duty of this Government to extend to them all the protection which may be within its power, or to retaliate for injuries done to them.

III. *Resolved,* That in the event the enemy shall, in revenge for such patriotic defense of their State by any of its citizens, seize upon and imprison, or otherwise injure other of its citizens not implicated in the particular acts for which such revenge may be taken, or shall pillage or destroy the property of any of our citizens, it will be the duty of this Government to take prompt notice of such acts of cowardly barbarity, and as far as may be within its power, to punish the perpetrators thereof, or to retaliate in such manner as may be most likely to deter the enemy from the repetition of such deeds.

IV. *Resolved,* That the Senate has learned with lively satisfaction that the President of the Confederate States has already given serious attention and grave consideration to the subject of several gross violations of the laws and usages of civilized war by the military authorities of the Government of the United States, and has already iniated measures tending to prevent their recurrence; and while the Senate responds with sympathy to the regret expressed by the President at the stern necessity which the enemy seems ruthlessly to force upon this Government of protecting its citizens by the bloody law of retaliation, it will give to the President its unfaltering support in the prompt execution of measures devised for the complete protection of our citizens in the exercise of the inalienable rights of self-defense.

V. *Resolved,* That the Committee on Military Affairs are instructed to enquire and to report whether any further, and if so, what legislation may be necessary to clothe the Executive with the amplest authority to act upon and carry out the intent and principles enumerated in these resolutions.

The resolutions having been read, Mr. YANCEY spoke as follows:

MR. PRESIDENT—I am fully impressed with the belief that the circumstances surrounding us call for the development of all our military power, and a resort to the sternest measures to deter the enemy from a cowardly and barbarous treatment of our people. I am not fully informed as to the opinions of the Executive as to the right of our citizens to wage individual hostilities against the invader for the protection of their State, their homes, and their liberties, but judging from the letter of the Secretary of War to the Hon. Senator from Missouri, [Mr. Clarke,] I incline to the opinion that the Executive is disposed either to deny that right or to suppress its exercise as impolitic. The country is in painful uncertainty upon the question, and I wish the matter to be settled by some solemn decision of Congress.

The first resolution announces as a fact that the war is waged by the United States against the citizens of the Confederate States as individuals, and states also, as a principle, that by the fundamental law of this Government, sovereignty rests in the people of each State alone, and that the Government is but their agent. Upon this fact and this principle I build up the conclusion that when one of the States is invaded for the purpose of destroying that sovereignty, and of confiscating the property and taking away the liberties of its people, each citizen is justified in attacking and slaying the invader wherever he may meet him, and by all the means the God of nature has put into his hands and which are known to civilized warfare.

The Secretary of War has said that by the customs of modern warfare war is to be considered as waged between governments—thereby implying, if not directly stating, that the people are not considered as parties to it. This might be very truly stated as to the wars of Europe between sovereign dynasties—where sovereignty is claimed to rest in the government only, and where the people are held as subjects. But it cannot, in my opinion, be correctly held as to a war of conquest waged against a government of the character of this, in which our peoples constitute the sovereignty, and government is nothing but the agent of these several sovereignties. In Europe it generally matters but little to the people which sovereign family rules over them, for their taxes are not lessened, nor their privileges increased as a general thing, by any result of war. They remain subjects under any event. But how different with us. In the event of our failure to maintain ourselves, not only is our property to be confiscated, but imprisonment and death, on a scale hitherto unknown, is threatened, and the right of self-government even is to be wrested from us.

It should also be borne in mind, that our enemy does not admit that we have a rightful government, either State or Confederate, deeming and treating our system of governments but as so many rebellious organizations, and their war, therefore, is both in

6

theory and in practice waged against each loyal citizen of the Confederacy as a rebel.

In confirmation of this, look to their military occupation of Kentucky, against the remonstrances of that State—to their course in Missouri, towards both its government and people— to their displacement of the authorities of Tennessee and Louisiana and of North Carolina, and to their governing of those States, as far as they can do so, as military provinces. Read their acts of confiscation and of threatened punishment of all our people by fine and imprisonment, and then look to their acts of murder, rape and robbery, wherever their armies occupy our soil.

In my opinion there can be no doubt that when a State is invaded, each of its citizens, as one of the sovereignty thus put in danger and thus directly assailed, has as much right to slay the invading foe as a sovereign Prince in Europe has to put on armor and war upon an invader of his principality. The doctrines of European warfare no more restrict him in the exercise of this right, than the doctrine of European sovereignty restricts him in the right of self-government—the right of secession— the right of revolution, all of which are alone recognized in our government. The exercise of such a right will also be of the greatest disadvantage to the enemy, who have their armies far from the residences of their people, and can therefore bring to their aid no counteracting policy of the kind, while it will be to us a strength as great, perhaps greater even, than that of our organized armies. History furnishes a noted example of the tremendous strength of a people entirely in arms for the defense of their homes. One of its most significant pages tells us that when Spain was invaded by the invincible legions of Napoleon, (invincible in regular combat) and had no organized forces to resist their occupancy of that country, the people of Spain, scorning submission and determining to resist subjugation to the dominion of France, took up arms, and in self-constituted bands, sallying forth from the forest, from the plain, from the valley, and from the mountain-tops, literally destroyed the armies of France in piece-meal operations. What though the gibbet and the halter, the dungeon and the musket-shot were threatened, and did, in fact, destroy thousands upon thousands of those patriots! Life to them was of no value without national liberty. Death had no terrors to those brave hearts, in defense of their firesides. I have, sir, sometimes been forced to contemplate the day when our organized efforts might be crushed by overwhelming numbers and for want of the material element of war. But should that day ever come, it will bring no despair of the cause to my mind as long as there exists a brave, united and patriotic people, to make of each hill-top a fort, of each pass an ambuscade, and of each plain a battle-field. Pass the resolutions, and you will at once give greater enthusiasm to each brave heart—increased strength to the determined will of our people.

The other resolutions provide for the protection of our citizens, who may thus act in defense of their State, and make it the duty of the Government to take such measures as will deter the enemy from acts of revenge on account of such action.

It is well known that the enemy has treated our citizens, not enrolled in the armies of the country, as outlaws and rebels. We do not come to this conclusion from such isolated facts as might be considered as but the outbreak of lawless soldiery under circumstances of peculiar temptation. The facts to sustain the charge are as numerous as the raids of the enemy, taking place over the entire region covered by their lines, from the seaboard to the far west, raids as brutal, and cowardly, and beastly as might be expected from the well established character of the Yankee people. They have been enacted for so long a time, that the enemy has become encouraged in the indulgence of his cowardly revenge against non-combatants for the disgraces inflicted upon him in the open field of war by our brave troops; and, in addition to his cruelties and beastly conduct to men, women and children, he has openly proclaimed, as one of the elements of hostility to us, the plunder of inoffensive people. Well authenticated history will show that whole villages of unresisting people have been given up to the unbridled lust of a brutal and cowardly soldiery by order of one of their commanders; while in numerous instances in the State of Virginia, daughters have been foully dishonored in the presence of their aged parents by commissioned officers of the enemy's army, and the broken hearted father shot down on his own hearth-stone for his brave but ineffectual efforts to defend the honor of his family. Sir, it is time that this Government should no longer repress the yearning of our people to take up arms to defend their homes, in such manner as may yet be consistent with their attempts to maintain their families by the ordinary pursuits in life. The rights they have at stake—the character of their Government—the object and the manner of the war waged upon them, all demand of this Senate and of every Department of this Government, the fullest approval of their right to do so, and the amplest guarantee for their protection in its exercise.

Painful as may be the alternative, we have no choice left us. Humanity itself—weeping humanity—demands a prompt and an unfaltering exercise of every right of the law of self-defense, both by our people and our Government.

It may bring the enemy with which we contend to be content with the exercise of the laws of civilized war; but if in his blind rage and maddened furor at being foiled by an inferior, braver and more skillful army than his own, he shall choose to retaliate for a just retaliation; if he has nerve enough to tread that terrible and bloody path, and to brave the powers and maledictions of the civilized world, he may be assured, should be assured by this Congress, that having counted the cost of this great movement for self-government, we shall not turn back, nor be deterred by any terrors from prosecuting it to a successful though it may be a most bloody conclusion.

Mr. YANCEY said that he had been betrayed into a more lengthy expression of his views than he had anticipated, and concluded by asking the Senate to act directly upon the propositions he had submitted.

250 copies of the resolutions were ordered to be printed, and they were made the order of the day for 25th August; and finally were placed upon the calendar of the secret session.

SECRET SESSIONS.

IN THE SENATE, on the 21st August, 1862, Mr. YANCEY gave notice of a motion to amend the rules of the Senate, so as to require a vote of two thirds of the Senators to go into secret legislative session. On the 22d August he addressed the Senate in favor of his motion, as follows:

Mr. PRESIDENT: The rules of the Senate, which I have moved to amend, make secrecy in legislation the rule, and open session the exception. The 43d rule which I have proposed should be stricken out, requires the Senate to go into secret session upon motion of a Senator, seconded by another. The 45th rule makes it the duty of the Senate to consider all questions relating to the public defense in secret session, unless determined otherwise by a secret vote. The effect of my amendments, if adopted, will be that all legislative sessions will be open to the public, except in such cases, as, in the opinion of two thirds of the Senate voting in open session by yeas and nays, the interests of the country shall require to be considered with closed doors.

On first taking my seat in the Senate, I called the attention of members to this subject, as an anomaly in republican government, but was disposed to yield and did yield my own views to the generally expressed opinion of Senators, that it was a wise policy under the circumstances, and had worked well. The subject, however, has engaged much of my attention and reflection during the recess, and I am now fully convinced that we have too much secrecy in our legislation, and that, as a matter of republican principle, it is clearly wrong to make secrecy the general rule of the Senate. I do not know, Mr. President, that the opinions of Senators have undergone any change on this subject, but I conceive it to be my duty to make an effort to bring back the Government to a more clearly defined republican track, and to place myself fairly on record before the public.

I do not doubt that, in times like these, there are matters which a wise prudence requires us to consider in secret. My proposed amendment leaves it in the discretion of the Senate— to be exercised, however, in open session—under its responsibility to the people, to consider such matters in secret. But, in my opinion, there are far fewer calls for the exercise of such discretion, than is generally supposed by Senators.

The reasons urged in support of secret sessions resolve themselves into two propositions:

1st. It is unwise to let the enemy know of our discussions.

2d. It is unwise to let our constituency know of our discussions.

I do not think, giving the fullest force to both propositions, that the doubtful benefit accruing from them, at all equals the injury done to public sentiment, by depriving the people of a knowledge of your proceedings.

It must be borne in mind that no military plans are devised here, no contemplated army movements are known to Senators. Financial questions with us would seem to need no secrecy. The whole world knows that we operate alone upon our credit with our own people. What is there then that requires secrecy as a general rule, in the wide range of legislation? You publish all your laws, military and financial. The chief results of your deliberation are made known. But you conceal from your constituents your individual action, your individual views. You conceal from them propositions which are rejected, and the names of those who propose and who reject them. You conceal from them the projectors of laws which are adopted, and of those who sustained or opposed them. You conceal from them the fact that plans were not proposed which, in their opinion. might have been wisely proposed and adopted. You conceal from them also that class of legislative action of the two houses which may have been vetoed by the Executive; and you leave them entirely ignorant as to the relative wisdom or independence of their Executive and their Representatives in such cases. These, in my opinion, constitute the great mass of matter kept from the public by secrecy; and these I would unveil to the scrutiny of our constituency. In doing so, I can see but little public evil which would result, on the contrary, much public good.

It is said, however, that sentiments sometimes expressed by Senators have a bad influence on the public mind. I do not think so. I have a far different view of the firmness and wisdom of the public mind. It has not been depressed by misfortune to our arms nor by loss of territory, but on the contrary has been influenced by such misfortune to renewed exhibition of courage, energy and patriotism. There was a time doubtless in which the public heart might have been discouraged by indiscreet speakers—the period immediately folllowing the acts of secession, when large minorities existed in nearly every State opposed to this movement, when public sentiment had not been consolidated in its favor—a time when the enlight. ened and patriotic leaders of the old Union party were overwhelmed with anxiety, lest lessons of conservative regard for the Union and hope in ultimate justice from the North had been too deeply engraved upon the hearts of that party—a time before we had learned to have confidence in each other, and to mutually understand the baseness and tyranny of the enemy.

But that time and its distrusts have passed away. I say it, fully weighing each word I use, that to-day we present to the world a greater unity in numbers, in confidence in each other, and in adherence to our cause, than our forefathers presented in the revolution—than the Yankees present to-day—than is to be found even in the well poised Government of Great Britain, or in any of the great powers of Europe. I further say it, with the fullest sense of its entire truth, and in no carping spirit, of course, for any department of the Government, that the great public sentiment of our people to-day is of a higher cast of revolutionary energy, wisdom and devotion than that of their Government agents. And the only fear Senators need entertain of the effect of giving publicity to their proceedings, is that there will be a stern demand that they eschew all reliance for success other than upon their constituency—and that they shall call more freely for men and means to carry this war into the enemy's country. Sir, on a memorable occasion in the history of this war, it did transpire that there had been, somewhere, in some Department of the Government—Legislative or Executive, an astoundingwant of comprehension of the magnitude of the crisis, and a consequent failure to provide for a proper defense of the country. I allude to the fall of Forts Henry and Donelson, and of Roanoke Island—to the rapid loss of Southern Kentucky, of Middle Tennessee, and of North Alabama. The public had been at ease since the battle of Manassas. Lured to repose and confidence by the quiet engendered by secrecy in their own Government—and by the apparent inertness of the foe, it deemed that all was well, and that the Government agents were as watchful, wise and energetic as the foe. But when, in February last, near half a million of the enemy rushed upon our borders and took possession of large sections of some of our most valuable territory and of the key to an immense extent of Atlantic coast, the people were aroused from their ease and shaken in their confidence, by finding that the country had neither men nor arms in the field at all adequate to its defense.

What facts on your secret journal—what discussion in your secret session, if given publicly to the world, were so well calculated to encourage the enemy as this publicly demonstated weakness in a most critical hour, and were so well calculated to depress and to demoralize our people.? And yet so far from demoralizing—from depressing—or discouraging our people, to the sudden call of the President " To arms ! " the Southwest arose in the might of a giant, and coming forth from hill top, valley and plain, the people with their rude weapons of war, immediately formed an army, and the enemy has been unable to advance one mile beyond the lines obtained by surprise, in unequal conflict, and is now retreating to his fortresses.

Now, sir, who is there will dare assert that, had the people known the true state of things from August '61 to February '62, this baneful repose of the Government would have been allowed such long continuance? Was their legislative representative at fault? He would have been aroused by the patriotic and enlightened energy of his constituents to the necessity of some attempt to put the country on a proper war footing. Was their executive representative at fault? Acted upon, both by the people's own expressed will and that of their Congress, he too, it may be supposed, would have been aroused to the necessity of lopping off the weak branches of his administration, and of exerting more energy to obtain both men and arms.

If men had been needed, they were in the country and ready to volunteer when fully apprised of the necessity. For instance, after these disasters, at the call of the President my own gallant State furnished eight regiments of volunteers in excess of her assigned quota. Were arms needed? In addition to a very large number of private arms, with which a large proportion of the late volunteers armed themselve, there were the vast storehouses of Europe, from which the Yankees drew, in six months, over half a million of good weapons; and which were equally accessible to us. Instead of being appalled by your expenditures for the war, the people, who pay that expenditure, are amazed at the parsimony of Cabinet calls for appro-

riations. They have the all that is at stake—liberty, life, property; and their chief demand, in which, in my opinion, they are
wiser than the Government, is that you spend more of their
property and risk more of their lives for the safety of their
liberties.

Such a spirit is not to be depressed or demoralized by a full
knowledge of your discussions. But it is urged that public
discussions will give rise to parties and to factions. Parties are
incident to institutions based on elective franchise; and it
has been a republican argument, that parties keep up a healthy
public sentiment, and aid to check improper assumption of power by those in office.

As to factions, I have but little fear of them, if you will let
in the healthful sunlight of an enlightened public opinion upon
your body. Far more likely to have factions generated in the
unhealthy shade of secret sessions—under the more poisonous
miasma which is generated in darkness, and which is dispelled
by the morning sun. In the years 1778, 1779 and 1790, before
the Constitution was formed, when our forefathers had no President, and governed the country by a single provisional body,
that body held secret sessions. In the Convention which
framed the Constitution. Col. Mason said: "The people will
not give their confidence to a secret journal—to the intrigues
and factions naturally incident to secrecy. If any one doubts
the existence of such a state of things in Congress, let him re-
fer to its journals of 1778, 1779 and 1790."

I have been considering this question, Mr. President, as a
policy. I come now to view it in its higher aspect, as related
to the fundamental principle upon which this Government is
founded—the elective franchise. The Executive and each
branch of Congress is elected. The right to elect involves approval or condemnation—involves a supposed know'edge of the
opinions and actions of the candidate upon public questions.
And yet what a farce—what a humbug—what perfection of fac-

tion will elections become indeed, when the constituency have no record upon the most momentous period of their Government action, by which to approve or to condemn a public servant, who is a candidate for re-election! By your own act you deprive your constituency of the means of an intelligent and patriotic exercise of the highest function of citizenship, and under such circumstances elections will become but a struggle of factions for the advancement of wicked, personal aspirations.

I move the adoption of my motion.

CONSCRIPTION.

In the Senate, on the 3d of September, Mr. Yancey offered the following amendment to the bill, reported by the Senate Committee on Military Affairs, to amend an Act entitled " An Act to provide for the public defense," approved 16th of April, 1862.

Strike out all after the enacting clause, and insert:

' That the President be, and is hereby authorized, and it shall be his duty to make requisition upon the Executive authorities of the several States of the Confederacy for their proper proportion or quota of—————:———troops, to be raised from citizens between the ages of 35 and 45, and to be received in companies of not less than 100, nor more than 120 men, officered under the laws of the State furnishing them. Said troops to be received into the service of the Confederate States for the term of three years or during the war, to be organized in such manner as the President may deem most conducive to the public interest, and in all respects to be considered as part of the army of the Confederate States.

Sec. 2. In the event any of the Governors of the several States shall fail or refuse to comply with said requisition, within thirty days after it shall have been made, the President in that event is hereby authorized, and it shall be his duty, to cause to be enrolled in the military service of the Confederate States all able bodied white men in the several States, not legally exempt from such service, who may be between the ages of 35 and 45 years, in addition to those subject to enrollment under the " Act further to provide for the public defense," approved 16th April, 1862, who shall be organized under the provisions of that Act:—Provided, that no officers, civil or military, of the governments of the States shall be enrolled, either under this Act or the Act to further provide for the public defense, approved 16th April, 1862: and Provided further, that all men now in the army over 45 years, of age shall be entitled to an immediate discharge within sixty days after the passage of this act.

On the 4th September, Mr. YANCEY said:

Mr. PRESIDENT—At the last session I voted for the Act, commonly called the Conscript Act, reported by the Committee on Military Affairs in conformity with the recommendation of the President, chiefly because of the necessity of keeping in the army, then menaced by superior numbers of the enemy, some seventy-five or eighty thousand experienced and brave soldiers, whose terms of service were expiring even while we were enacting the law. Had it not been for that controlling necessity, I believe another mode of raising men for our armies would have been adopted. That reason—that hard necessity does not exist now. Our armies are driving the enemy before them, and we can deliberate upon and adopt the best means of recruiting them, without doing violence to the feelings or prejudices of any.

The attempt to put that law in force has called forth solemn protests, from at least two of the Governors of the States, against its constitutionality, and has in some other quarters produced irritation on account of its hardship and supposed violation of State's rights. In one instance an actual collision between the authorities of a sovereign State and of the Confedecy, was alone prevented by the prudence and moderation of the President, for which he deserves well of the country.

I have not had, and do not now have, a particle of doubt as to the constitutionality of that law. I have not read or heard of any argument against it, which I conceived tenable; and in proposing now to raise troops for our army in some other mode, if practicable, it is not that conscription is unconstitutional, but that it is wise, in my opinion, to act, as far as possible, in harmony with the authorities of the several States, so long as we can do so consistently with our duty to the common cause. If one or more of the sovereign States conceive that conscription is wrong, and yet are unwilling to furnish all the troops required through State agency, the main object being to obtain the troops, it seems to me to be both wise and dignified to accept them at the hands of the States, and to forego our right to go into a State and to enroll the men "individually." We should remember that State sovereignty, which in some respects is the strongest, may yet become the weakest point in our organic system. We should remember that, no matter what may be the logic of our position, the States, in our acknowledged view of their relation to this government and each other, have the right to judge for themselves, in the last resort; and on a question of the invasion of their rights by this government, are likely to decide that question from their own stand-point, and in favor of their own interests. 'It seems to me that no statesman would, without the sternest necessity, force such an issue upon them. In war an agrieved State may yield its judgment simply because of external pressure, and the danger of intestine division.

Such was the action on the Conscript act of the Governor of this State. But the matter does not and cannot pass away, with a mere protest. When the war ceases—when this external pressure is removed and peace gives occasion for the full development of State sovereignty and resources—such collisions, such temporary submission, favored by circumstances, are remembered as humiliations; they are like old wounds, and occasion a jealous and watchful conduct towards the Confederate Government which inflicted them, and tend to breed parties, which, in the end, may disrupt the Government.

I desire, in all my action as a Senator, to give as little occasion for remembrances of this kind as possible.

Senators speak of prosecuting the war with energy. Energy which arises from the smooth and harmonious action of all the parts of our complex Government, in favor of a common cause, is one thing—and, in my opinion, the one thing to be desired; but that energy of one Department, which produces discord between the State Governments and that of the Confederate States, is another thing, which, in my opinion, is most deeply to be deplored and to be avoided. The former I desire to produce by the substitute I offer. It is a peace offering. The occasion is propitious for offering it. Our armies are victorious and the people and authorities of the several States, filled with patriotic fervor and hope, will promptly respond to whatever call for aid their common agent—the Confederate Government may make.

The first section of the substitute authorizes a call upon the States to furnish each their proportion of such number of men as you may designate, between 25 and 45 years old, to be furnished in companies within 30 days, and to be officered according to the laws of the State.

The second section provides, in the event of the failure of a State to respond, that the President shall proceed to enroll all between 35 and 45. The substitute gives to each State the opportunity and privilege of furnishing its quota, officered by itself. Who can doubt that the opportunity will be seized upon with alacrity by each State to exhibit its energy and patriotism. Why, sir, when the last call was made upon my State for twelve regiments, she furnished over twenty full regiments. The substitute leaves the conscript act in full force; and by means of that act, properly administered, after you have duly amended it and the exempt law, you will be able to raise men enough between 18 and 35 to fill up the old regiments to at least 700 or 800 men each.

There is another difference between the substitute and the bill of the committee. The latter only authorizes the President to enroll the men. If he sees proper, under that bill he may delay doing so, or not do so at all.

Now I call attention to the message of the President. He says events may happen which will render it necessary to have the men, &c. He seems to intimate that at present there is no need of more men. If that is the opinion of the President, then, as a Senator, I differ from him, and express my opinion that we need the men now. We need to go to work at once to raise and equip and subsist them. It is true, our armies, are everywhere victorious, from the Mississippi to the Potomac; but we need to keep them in the path of victory—we need so to strengthen them that they shall rush through the Yankee capital, blow up every vestige of its public buildings, and pass on into the heart of the enemy's great cities, and in the midst of his treasures, and in the citadels of his power dictate a peace. I have ever been of the opinion that it was unwise to permit the war to have its seat and progress in the midst of our institutions; and that while we should assail the liberties and existence of no other people, we should defend our own when assailed on the very hearthstones of our assailants. We want no protracted war; we want peace—the dearest, most valued privilege of a Christian people. To have peace, we want a numerous army that can force it. Therefore, Mr. President, in the substitute I have offered, I have not only authorized the President to call for, or to enroll these troops, but I have made it "his duty" to do so.

In another particular the substitute differs from the bill of the committee. The latter does not touch the delicate question made by the Governor of Georgia, and leaves the question as it stood before. In my opinion, the Conscript act could well be construed, taken in connection with the Exemption act, as exempting all State officers. I think, indeed, that they are not liable to conscription by virtue of the organic law of the Constitution. I look upon the exemption act, as far as it relates to Governors, Judges, members of Congress, as simply declaratory of Constitutional law—and not as, in fact, exempting those officers per se. But as the question has been raised, we should meet it and not leave it in doubt. My substitute does so, and declares that no civil or military officer of a State enrolled by the President. I hold that we have no power to do so—that it is a reserved right of a State to keep perfect its own State organization. That organization is executive, legislative and judicial. You have as much power to trench upon and curtail all of these departments of State government as you have to take a Justice of the Peace, or a Constable and put him in your army. It has been proposed in the Senate to-day, in considering the exemption bill, to enroll Justices of the Peace as soldiers in your army; and the Senator from Georgia has advocated the power to do so in an ingenious and elaborate speech. He declares that your power to raise armies is only limited by your necessity, and that you can enroll every member of this body and every member of a State government, if you see proper to do so. With such sentiments declared in the Senate, it is time that by some solemn vote this principle should be passed upon, and in my opinion should be repudiated by this body.

This Government I hold to be an agent of the States composing it—established to secure to each State and the people thereof the blessings of constitutional liberty—and that the great mass of the personal rights and liberties of the citizen are derived from the State constitutions.

The States are the creators of this governmental agency, and under our system, as now organised, can each separate itself from it, when, in its judgment, it may think it best to do so; and there is no power in the Confederate Government to say nay.

The State governments, then, are an essential part of the complex system of government known as the Confederate States. They are essentially necessary to its existence and its practical working. Without them there can be no Senate. I sit here to-day as a citizen of Alabama [not as a citizen of the Confederate States] chosen by the government of my State.

Without State Governments there can be no House of Representatives, because there can be no electors of that House—they being such as the State Governments designate.

Yet, although these things be so, the Senator from Georgia [Mr. HILL,] says that he boldly meets my proposition and avers that under the war-making power Congress can enroll every judicial officer of a State, from Justice of the Peace to the Chief Justice upon the supreme bench—can enroll every member of Congress—and as one reason therefor has brought into the Senate Lincoln's great reason for all his usurpations—that the 'National life is in danger.'

[Mr. HILL declined saying anything that would justify Lincoln's usurpations.]

Far be it from me to make such an assertion of the distinguished Senator; but he has urged that "the National Life" was in danger, and that our war power was unlimited, and therefore we could conscript State officers. Mr. President, I here enter my solemn protest against the introduction into our political vocabulary of such a phrase as "the National Life." Sir, we have no national life. "National Life" is but another term for Sovereignty. A nation is a Sovereign State; the Confederacy is not a Sovereign State. This Government, as to foreign nations, is a Confederacy, and may be termed by them national. As between itself and its creators, the States, it is but an agent and in no sense national. It has no national life to defend. Its province—its sole province, is to defend Constitutional Liberty—the Constitutional liberties of the States and of the people of the States. Its agency is to guard, preserve, and perpetuate those liberties. To that end it has given to it the power to make war—to raise armies; but how absurd to construe that power into a power to crush, to destroy, or in any way to curtail any of those rights of its creators—the States— or of the liberties of a single citizen of the States. If the principle is yielded that Congress can, under the war power, destroy or conscript the civil or military officers of a sovereign State, then that State Government, during a time of war, exists only by the will of Congress—either to be suspended altogether, or to exist in a maimed and inefficient manner. If such a principle is correct, then it follows that the Confederate Government is of greater value and more sacred than the States and the liberties of citizens of the States.

Mr. President, I meet this assumption of power on the threshold. I deny *in toto* that the Confederate Government is superior to and of more value than the reserved rights of the States and of the people thereof. I deny *in toto* that the war power is paramount to the civil power, either of the Confederate or State Governments. All history teaches us, it is true, that in time of war the civil shrinks in the back ground before the fiercer bearing and more energetic action of the war power. Such, in fact, is the state of things in the Confederacy to-day. Even in the very citadel of the civil power its chosen guardians choose to yield to the usurpations of the leaders of armies and to palliate if not justify them. I am not one of those. I here assert that the war power is but one of the means belonging to the civil power, to be used to maintain and defend and preserve the great elements of civil governments; that the raising of armies, the conduct of the war, the duration of the war, are all within the scope and control of the legislative power—the only power which is supreme in this government. We are the masters of that power of war, and it is to be made subservient to our will. Practically, I admit that in parts of the country it has been the reverse. We have a General who, by military orders, assumes a military censorship over the press. We have a General who declares martial law over whole States, and has even carried his usurpation so far as to abrogate the municipal government of one of our large towns and to appoint a military governor over its inhabitants. More monstrous usurpations never were practised by any of the Stuarts. This is that West Point despotism, which, in its arrogance, deems the people incapable of furnishing a good officer to command their volunteers, or even of governing themselves in time of war. It is the result of an exclusive military education, which cultivates the idea that the glory of arms is the great glory of life.

It is time that Congress was gravely considering this state of things. It is time that West Point despotism was crushed in the conduct of the army, as well as driven out of this hall, where it seeks to obtain a footing.

It is on account of the responsibility which I conceive these facts have thrown upon us, that I have introduced a proviso into the substitute that no civil or military officer of a State shall be conscripted. I believe, as a matter of fact, that there is but little use, during these troublesome times, for many magistrates and constables and clerks in the States. But it is not within our province to reach the evil. It is the privilege of each State to regulate its own government. It is in their jurisdiction to dispense with them. If they do, they then fall within our power to conscript. But I will be the last one to tear them from the protection of State sovereignty.

Neither are we so hard pressed, Mr. President, that we should be driven to exercise this power, even if we possessed it. Our armies are now victorious everywhere. They have been so for months. It is the result of superior generalship and the superior fighting qualities of our armies.

It is true, it is wise now to commence recruiting, for we have hundreds of thousands of our people to spare; but it is equally true that we can only arm and subsist a certain number, and we can easily raise that number and yet not encroach upon the officers of any of the State Governments. I hope that my amendment will be adopted.

The Exemption bill being under consideration, Mr. DORTCH, of North Carolina, moved to amend the bill so that Justices of the Peace should be liable to conscription. On the 10th September, 1862, Mr. YANCEY addressed the Senate, upon that motion, as follows:

MR. PRESIDENT: The Senator from North Carolina proposes that Justices of the Peace in the several States shall be enrolled as conscripts in the army of the Confederate States—at the same time giving notice that he will offer other amendments, making other State officers liable to enrollment under the conscript act. The Senators from Georgia, [Mr. HILL,] from Mississippi, [Mr. PHELAN] and from Kentucky, [Mr. SIMMS] have supported that amendment, and have asserted the power of Congress to enroll as conscript soldiers in the army every officer of a State, whether Judicial Legislative or Executive, and also every officer under the Confederate Government, whether Judicial Legislative or Executive, with but a single exception—and that exception the President of the Confederate States. The enrollment or exemption of a few thousands, filling the humble but useful office of Justice of the Peace, can be of but little moment compared with the vast fundamental change in the character of this Government which practical legislation upon such principles must bring about. Legislation upon the principles which have been thus distinctly avowed and elaborately argued would, in my opinion, utterly subvert the limited Constitutional Government, which the people have been at so much pains to establish and have exhibited so much patriotic sacrifice and energy to defend, and would effectually erect upon its ruins a purely military Government. So thinking, I should be unjust to all the principles upon which I have acted in the past, and dirilect to the duty I owe to the State which I in part represent here, and to the oath I have taken to preserve and defend the constitution, if I were to permit the avowal of such doctrines to pass unchallenged. If this amendment had been proposed and passed upon without debate, Mr. President, it might have thus become one of the facts in legislative history of comparitively small moment, and not justly held to be a precedent. But its introduction has been supported by grave and apparently maturely considered opinions of Senators from three of the thirteen States of the Confederacy, and has led to a more lengthened and dignified debate than any other that has occurred in this body since my connection with it. Such a debate, upon such an issue, in my opinion, will mark the action of the Senate upon it as one of the great landmarks in legislative construction of the constitution; and as the question passes into history, its footprints will be gravely scrutinized and considered hereafter as indicating the progress of this government either in the march of a well understood constitutional policy, leading us on to an assured political and commercial greatness as a free people—or in that broad and well beaten path, from which the wrecks of government that for centuries have strewn it could not deter us—a path which leads to absolutism in the person of some mighty and unscrupulous military genius. This being the case, our decision is of the gravest importance, not only for to-day, but for all time. Our action then should be clearly defined, and leave no room for doubt as to our views of the comparative dignity and extent of the civil and of the war powers of this Government.

Mr. President, the question is not an abstract one, which can be postponed without detriment. It presses upon you as a practical question, requiring legislative solution. Signs are not lacking that the war power is quietly usurping the powers of both State and Confederate Governments. All history teaches us that, in times of war, the more modest and less showy civil powers of government yield and shrink before the fiercer bearing and more pretensions and swelling demeanor of the war power.

In our own case, so great is the patriotic fervor of the people —so ardent their devotion to the cause—so unselfish their sacrifices of property, of ease, aye! of life itself, in promotion of the common weal—that they are loth to question any act that is designed to advance the common interest, no matter how strange or startling to them as a mere question of power. So far has this generous support of our generals gone, that it requires some moral courage to sustain any one who thinks it his duty to say "eternal vigilance is the price of liberty." Hence, this generous confidence, while it deters many a watchful patriot from doing his whole duty, has actually been seized upon as a defense by some who have violated civil liberty in the exercise of military power, and their acts have been justified because the people are quiet.

But, Mr. President, this should not influence Senators in their action here. Here we act upon our solemn oaths to see to it that the Republic suffers no detriment. Here we are as watchmen to tell our constituents "what of the night." Here we are put upon our consciences, without fear or favor of the people, to do our duty—our whole duty—not according to the "general welfare," nor to that other dangerous plea of all usurpers, "necessity"—but according to the written law of the Constitution, which has been placed in our hands as our only power of attorney to act at all. Under such influences, as one of these watchmen, I say there are already signs that a change from a civil government, with constitutional checks and balances, to a military absolutism, is in progress. What are the facts to sustain so startling an assertion? I repeat a few of them:

A military commander of a department has declared martia l law in his district, and has muzzled the free press within it.

The first step towards despotism is invariably to suppress that watchful friend of civil liberty—the free press; and the next is to suppress the civil law which would rescue a victim from lawless arrest and check all encroachments upon the people's rights.

Another military commander is solemnly charged—and it is a matter of inquiry in this body—with having executed a citizen without a trial, either under civil or military law. The same commander has superceded the municipal law by his own military edict; has displaced the authorities elected by the people, under the sovereign law of their State, and has placed over them an officer of his own choosing. And, as if these startling usurpations were not sufficient to satisfy this craving of the military to drive all civil power into obscurity—in fact, to banish it from the land—here in the Senate, the chosen temple of State sovereignty, one of the tribunals upon which it would be supposed the civil power could safely repose, Senators from several sovereign States are to be found who deliberately assert that Congress can suspend and supercede all civil governments, both Confederate and State; for they assert that, under the clauses giving Congress the power to declare and conduct the war, it can coerce every officer as well as citizen of the State governments, and every officer of the Confederate government, save the President, to serve in the regular army of the Confederate States as a soldier, so long as it may see fit to carry on the war.

Mr. President, if there are any within our land so misled as to desire to overthrow our present form of government, and to establish upon its ruins a central despotism, led by a dictator, they could not desire to have more effective aid in accomplishing their unhallowed designs than these Senators no doubt unwittingly lend to them. It is a most startling fact, and history will record it as one of the most strange in its annals, that in the first Senate assembled under a constitution which declares that it was formed by each State "acting in its sovereign and independent character," to "establish justice, insure domestic tranquility, and secure the blessings of liberty" to themselves and the posterity of their people—and in the first session of that Senate, Senators could be found, in the name of Liberty, to advocate the erection of the military power into such a supremacy that it would absorb and destroy all the State governments, and all the legislative power of the Confederate government— thus securing to the sword an unchecked dominion over a people who had seceded from the Lincoln usurpation for the sole purpose of preserving their liberties under their several State governments. Strange, too, that while thus severing their connection with that Lincoln usurpation on account of encroachments upon the rights of their citizens, any intelligent man should be found comprehending and approving the nature of the contest, who should follow, in his zeal to prosecute this war, the very footsteps of that Lincoln despotism. Lincoln and Seward proclaimed that the war power, the same in the Federal as in the Confederate constitution, justified the suppression of the municipal authorities of Baltimore and their imprisonment in Fort Lafayette. They thought that the press was too free in its criticism upon their acts, and they crushed its freedom and imprisoned its editors. They thought that the Judiciary should be subordinate to the war power, and they placed sentinels at the doors of the Judges, and disregarded their writs. They thought that independent State governments were stumbling blocks in their progress to military absolutism —were "absurdities"—and they imprisoned the members of the Legislature of a sovereign State.

And what were their special pleas for this effectual and rapid transformation of a constitutional government into a practical despotism which did not allow its decrees to be questioned?

One plea was that so ardently advanced by the Senator from

Kentucky, [Mr. Simms] in defense of the proposition to seize and coerce an officer of the civil government of a State into the army of the Confederacy—that it would be "absurd" to suppose that the constitution conferred upon Congress the power to wage war, and yet prohibited it from forcing a State officer to do duty as a private?

[Mr. Simms, of Ky.—The constitution nowhere gives Congress power to raise and support armies for the overthrow of the State government, but it does give this power to Congress, * "to protect each State against invasion." The language of the constitution is, "Congress shall protect each of them (the States) against invasion." The war in which we are now engaged, and the armies we are now raising and supporting are for that very purpose. If the whole physical power of the Confederacy be required in the military service to successfully "protect the State against invasion," I hold that Congress not only has power, but that it is made its highest duty by the constitution itself, to exercise that power to the full extent demanded by the exigencies of the occasion. I am, therefore, for conscripting magistrates into the military service, not for the purpose of overthrowing the State government, but for the purpose of preventing their enslavement and overthrow by a foreign invader.

For the constitution to declare "Congress shall protect each State against invation," and then declare that it shall not have power to raise a sufficient force to do it, is to say that the same constitution which declares that "Congress shall protect the State against invasion," also denies to. Congress the power to do the *very* thing it declares Congress *shall* and ought to do. Such a construction, I hold, would be enough to stamp the instrument *an absurdity*, and more than enough to stamp its authors with a stupidity incapable of understanding their own purpose.]

Mr. Yancey continued :

It seems, Mr. President, that I did not misapprehend the Senator. He repeats that such a limitation on the war power as will prevent the government from forcing an officer of a State government to serve in the army is an absurdity and a weakness of which the framers of the constitution could not be guilty. Precisely the same reasoning, if it can be called such, was used by Lincoln as to our right to secede from his government—and to his right to suppress what he called disloyal municipalities and State governments, and to imprison judges and editors of a free press. Another plea which Lincoln used to support his numerous usurpations and acts of tyranny, was that used here, by the Senator from Georgia—the necessity of preserving the National Life—as if there could be, in a free constitutional government, a national life that was antagonistic to the sovereign rights or life of a free State, or of a free citizen of such a State.

Another plea used by the authorities of the United States, in their internal war upon the personal rights of their own citizens and upon the sovereign rights of their own States, was that so vehemently urged here by the Senator from Mississippi, [Mr. Phelan] in behalf of his view that this Congress can coerce into its armies all the officers of the several States, and even the members of this body—the unlimited extent of the power of Congress over all other powers delegated by the States or reserved by them, in the conduct of the war.

[Mr. Phelan here disclaimed that he was one of those who made a mere general reference to the " war power " in showing the canstitutionality of any special measure. On the contrary he had disclaimed any such general reference as dangerous in principle and pointless as proof. A reference so indefinite, he had declared, was of no more force in proving the constitutionality of a special measure than a similar reference by its title to any other writing. Every power, claimed under the constitution, must be established by special clauses; and in his argu-

ment to show that Congress had power to exact military service of a State officer, he had referred to the special clauses by
which, he thought, it was granted.]

Mr. YANCEY—I have not, then, misapprehended the Senator.
He reasserts an unlimited right of Congress to coerce every citizen.. He only explains that he derives it from special clauses,
and not from a general reference to the war power. I mention
these coincidences between statesmen of different and antagonistic governments, not with a view of showing any common
design to destroy public liberty, but to warn Senators lest in
their patriotic zeal to strengthen their Government in the pros-
ecution of the war, they lay the foundation for an eventual destruction of the Government itself, and of all that vast mass of
personal and State rights which it is the sole object of the war
to secure and perpetuate. If the lessons of history, teaching
by example, are not too weak to be heard amidst the din of the
conflict, surely the more recent and striking example furnished
by our enemies because of their effect upon the struggle, should
cause Senators to pause in any course which would seem to en-
dorse and justify those usurpations and stultify ourselves by pur-
suing the like line of conduct. If there is anything in our form
of government which checks the unlimited expansion of the
war power, and reserves from seizure either State or Confederate civil rights—and Senators will persist in considering
such checks and reservations absurdities or weaknesses, let
them consider that thus it has been maturely and considerately
determined by the States. Sufficient to every legislator should
it be that over the whole fundamental power of our complex
government it is thus written. Enough for you should be the
wisest and most potent of all reasoning—*ita est scripta lex.* Thus
is the law written, and thus we are sworn to observe it.

But we are earnestly adjured not to let the constitution stand
in our way, when it is necessary to put every man in the field
in order to resist subjugation by the Lincoln despotism; and

that when the war is over we can return to the constitutional government. Mr. President, I here solemnly state my conviction, that it is far better for a free people to be vanquished in open combat with the invader than voluntarily to yield their liberties and their constitutional safeguards to the stealthy progress of legislative and executive usurpations towards the establishment of a military dictatorship. When a people have lost faith in the power of free government to defend their liberties, and lost that high courage and tried virtue which can wrestle with danger and meet disasters with fortitude—when in cowardly search of ease they discard the onerous and trying duties of self government, and throw themselves and their all into the arms of a vigorous despotism of their own choosing, in nine cases out of ten that people are lost—lost forever. The recuperative energy and virtue which would be required to throw off the shackles which they had thus placed upon their own limbs would be wanting, and they would undergo ages of suffering, before a new race of men could be born equal to a task of such magnitude. No, sir. Far better, in every particular, if they are to be governed by a despotism—if free constitutional government is to be overthrown, that it be overthrown by an open enemy, and if they are to be governed by a despotism, that it shall be after being vanquished in the conflict of arms. Virtues grow by trial; the virtues of courage, of patriotism, of love of liberty, are not uprooted by the triumph of an enemy, or by defeat at the hand of a foe. The world's history is full of the noble truth—the stern, bloody, practical truth which poetry has seized and almost consecrated as its own by reason of the amber of sweet numbers in which it has embalmed it—

" Freedom's battle once begun,
Bequeathed by bleeding sire to son,
Though baffled oft, is ever won!"

There is hope for a people who are crushed by superior power, in their brave struggle for the right. There is no hope for a people, so destitute of courage and virtue and wisdom as to flee to a despotism to render their conflict with an invader the easier. I therefore repudiate all idea that we can safely abandon any of the safeguards of our liberties in order more successfully to contend with our invaders.

Mr. President, I have said that this amendment and the principles upon which it has been supported, if carried into practical legislation, will destroy both the State and Confederate Governments, and will erect the Executive into a Military Dictatorship.

I now proceed to sustain that proposition.

In considering this question, it must be borne in mind that this is not a consolidated Government; but that the powers of this Confederacy are limited and delegated, and that all the powers of government are distributed between this and the several State Governments.

There are seven articles in the Confederate Constitution. I assert that the exercise of such powers by Congress will destroy the provisions of six of these articles, will thus destroy the various powers delegated to Congress which make this a constitutional civil government, and will leave the executive and war power without the checks and balances so wisely provided to keep it subordinate to the civil and legislative power.

In the first article are provisions that the Legislature of a State has power to prescribe who shall be voters for members of the House of Representatives; shall choose members of the Senate, and prescribe the times, places and manner of their election; that the State executive shall issue writs of election to fill vacancies in House of Representatives; and which reserve to a State the right to keep troops to resist invasion in time of war. Every one of these provisions can and would be destroyed by Congress assuming the powers contended for by the Senators from Georgia [Mr. Hill] and from Mississippi [Mr. Phe-

LAW], the power to place in the army for three years the members of the State Legislature and the Executive, through whose action alone can Representatives and Senators be elected, and the power to enroll as conscripts the militia officers of a State, and the militia, when called out by a State to resist its invasion.

Texas has a regiment of rangers now in her service to protect her borders; Virginia has a large body of her militia to protect her insulted territory. In my opinion, Congress cannot touch a man of either under the conscript law; although I believe that Congress can provide for calling forth the militia to repel invasion; and in such a case the States would be bound to send the militia in obedience to that clearly delegated power.

There is another class of provisions in the first article which the assumption of such powers by Congress as are contended for would render null and devoid. These Senators say distinctly that Congress has power to enroll every member of Congress as privates in the army for three years or more. Let us see the effect. The 1st article provides that all the legislative power shall be vested in Congress; that it shall meet once a year; that the House alone shall impeach an officer; that the Senate shall try impeachments; that members shall be free from civil or military arrests—save for treason, felony or breach of the peace and that all bills for raising revenue shall originate in the House. In addition to all this, there are nineteen distinct powers specially delegated to Congress in that article, six of which relate to the war power. To enroll members of Congress in the army would destroy the legislative branch of the Government, and would render Congress unable to exercise those powers and perform those duties; would take from the people of the States their voice in managing the General Government; would take from the States the representation of their sovereignty in this Government; would place the revenue in the hands of the Executive—would give him the purse as well as the sword. Further, the suppression of Congress, by its enrollment in the army, would destroy the only power which could impeach and try the Executive for usurpation.

Let us now examine the 2d article. It provides that the President shall be elected by electors every six years, chosen as the State Legislature may direct. It gives to him the power of appointment of officers subject to confirmation or rejection by the Senate. He can make treaties by and with the advice and consent of the Senate. He shall give information of the state of the Confederacy to Congress. He shall be removed from office by impeachment. But these Senators say that Congress has the power to destroy the State Legislatures, which prescribe the appointment of electors—has power to destroy the Senate, which can reject his appointees, and can reject his treaties, and which can remove him from office by impeachment. When all this has been done, there will be an Executive without the check of the legislative power, without the fear of the high court of impeachment—an Executive to raise money at will—to put up and put down at will—to make alliances with foreign powers, to maintain him in his one man power, without consultation or draw back from any quarter, and to keep the control of Government, as there will be no power in existence to elect his successor and dispute his term of office.

Let us examine the 3d article. It provides that the judicial power shall be vested in supreme and other courts, and that judges shall hold office during good behavior—that they shall preside over civil and criminal trials of prescribed character.

But these Senators declare that Congress has power to suspend that article—to render it of no effect—to take the judges from the bench and enroll them as soldiers under military rule —to deprive them of the dignities and privileges of their high office, no matter how irreproachable their life! The Chief Justice is required to preside in the Senate if the President is tried by impeachment. But although the President may have bribed members to destroy the civil functions of government, and may have constitutionally arrested and forced State authorities and all Congress and the Judiciary into his army, and therefore had assumed all the powers of government and be liable to be tried for treason, there will be found no House to impeach—no Senate to try him—no Chief Justice to preside—all will be forced under the principles so recklessly avowed here by the Senators from Georgia [Mr. HILL], from Mississippi [Mr. PHELAN], and from Kentucky [Mr. SIMMS], into subserviency under the mailed hand of a military Dictator, that has grown into being under the pleas of "necessity," and of the "unlimited" nature of the war power.

Under the 4th article the Confederate States guarantee to every State a republican form of government, and upon application of the Executive they protect it against domestic violence. Under the principles of these Senators, what becomes of this valuable provision? The Government of the Confederate States, so far from affording that guarantee, will have destroyed every vestige of republicanism in both State and General Government. It will have destroyed the Legislature, the Executive and the Judiciary of each State—it will have left it a prey to anarchy, or, what is more probable, each will have become a province of a military ruler, governed by one of his traps.

The spirit, the vitality, the essence of our republican system will in every particular have been effectually crushed. And when, in such an event the citizen—not then, but once the citizen of a free government—shall seek the sacred places where his State sovereignty was enshrined, and shall find the Executive chair vacant, and the mace of Executive authority broken —when he shall stray still further into the temple of State sovereignty and find the bench of justice no longer occupied, and the sacred ermine torn and trampled under the feet of military despotism—the very altars of his liberties desecrated and cast down—pray tell us, sir, what it will be to him that you did this from "necesssity"—to preserve the National life—from a fear of Lincoln hordes—from an opinion that you had a right to do it—what to him will be your desire to be successful in war, when success in war is based on a destruction of the very rights for which alone he was willing to incur its horrors and its dangers?

I pass over the 5th Article as of comparatively little importance to the 6th. The last two provisions are the most important in the whole Constitution—yet they were not devised by the wise men who framed that instrument in Convention. After they had sent it to the States for their consideration, a citizen of this ancient Dominion, far sighted and with a thorough knowledge of government and its workings as taught in history, had them, amongst others, proposed as amendments to the Constitution, and they were adopted. They constitute the grand beacon lights to every benighted or puzzled statesman by which to guide the bark of State. By their light there can be no excuse even for a blind man for not correctly reading this Constitution. They speak a language of warning, of instruction and reproof to the Senator from Mississippi (Mr. Phelan) who from certain special clauses, deduced the power of Congress to destroy or render null and of no effect nearly every other delegated power in that instrument, and to disparage, if not destroy, nearly every right retained and reserved by the States. I read them:

"The enumeration in the Costitution of certain rights shall not be construed to deny or disparage others retained by the people of the several States.

"The powers not delegated to the Confederate States by the Constitution, nor prohibited by it to the States, are reserved to the States respectively, or to the people thereof."

Now I put it to the Senate. Have not a few specified rights as to the conduct of the war power been so construed by the Senators who have advocated this amendment as "to deny or disparage the right of State Government which was 'retained' by the people of the several States?" Can those Senators deny that they have done so? Have they not so construed the few war powers as effectually to suppress the judiciary, the legislative and the Executive departments of the State Governments, if their principles should be fully acted upon by this Congress? Does any Senator pretend that the power of legislation upon domestic relations among citizens of a State has been delegated to Congress, or has been prohibited by the States? Not one. Then it is a reserved power of the States respectively. And if a reserve power, then, says the Constitution, "You shall not construe certain delegated rights," &c. Yet Senators have, without due reflection, I must suppose, done that very prohibited thing.

I have thus, Mr. President, performed my task. I have shown that the construction put by some Senators upon this war power is utterly at variance with six of the seven articles of the Constitution, and, if adopted and acted upon by Congress, will crush all civil power, destroy two out of the three great departments of the Government—namely: the legislative and judicial departments—will also destroy all the State Governments and will erect the limited Constitutional Executive into an absolute despotism—a pure military dictatorship. As I have so often alluded to the Executive, I here take occasion to say that, though differing on some matters with the President, I have no fears of his assuming unconstitutional power. Educated and living a strict constructionist, I believe his heart sympathises with his head, and that no more determined opponent of usurpation will be found in the Confederacy.

What is the reason urged for this assumption by Congress of unlimited war power? Necessity—blood-covered, liberty-despoiling, "necessity"—stained with the crimes of ages, and yet dripping with the fresher blood of a republic which, it may be no treason to wish, had received a happier fate.

But, Mr. President, "necessity" cannot justly be urged at this time for the perpetration of so heinous a crime against our own liberties—none more unpropitious for such an excuse as this bright period in the history of the war. Though hard pressed in the spring, when surprised and unprepared, the wonderful recuperative energy and ready resources of the Southern people have raised and equipped an army in the very presence of the three quarters of a million of armed and disciplined enemies; and those armies have driven back the enemy from all his fortified holds on our borders, and have routed him on several well contested fields, and now hang threatening over his capitol, and along his undefended frontier. Yet, strange to say, this is the hour chosen for an onslaught upon the dearest principles of the Southern people—upon the chief principle for which they separated from the Government of the United States, and upon which they have built up this Confederacy—the right to preserve intact the reserved rights of the States—the right to resist usurpation of those rights by the Federal Government.

Mr. President, I do not believe we are weakened for war by too much constitutional liberty. I have full faith in this complicated and limited Government to carry us safely through this war. Its strength, however, lies in the most careful observance of the rights of each department of the Government and of each State. Its greatest weakness is in a disposition to assume powers from a mischievous and fallacious idea that they are necessary to our safety. Such assumption is more to be feared, more dangerous, in my opinion, than are a million of Yankee bayonets. Let there be mutual respect for the rights of each and all—and there will result a harmony and an energy and a power that will secure to us all we value in constitutional government.

APPOINTMENT OF BRIGADIER GENERALS.

In the Senate, September 8th, Mr. Yancey introduced a bill to regulate the nomination and appointment of Brigadier Generals, so as to apportion them among the several States according to the number of troops furnished by each. The bill was referred to the Judiciary Committee, who reported it back with the following report:

The Committee on the Judiciary, to whom was referred "A Bill to regulate the nomination and appointment of Brigadier Generals," have had the same under consideration and ask leave to report:

The Constitution provides that the President "shall nominate, and by and with the advice and consent of the Senate, shall appoint ambassadors, other public ministers and consuls, judges of the Supreme Court, and all other officers of the Confederate States, whose appointments are not herein otherwise provided for, and which shall be established by law."

By this clause of the Constitution, the right of nomination, in the opinion of the committee, is given exclusively to the President. The power of appointment is given to the President, controlled by the advice and consent of the Senate only. In the matter of appointments, therefore, the Senate is an advisory Executive body, and in that capacity may exercise a regulating and restraining influence, power and discretion; and may appropriately take into consideration the relation of the officer proposed to the troops to be commanded, and to the citizens for whose immediate benefit his functions are to be employed.

But the Congress, as a legislative body, consisting of the Senate and House of Representatives, have no constitutional authority, in the opinion of the committee, to regulate or interfere with executive discretion in making nominations or appointments. The control of the Congress over appointments is confined to the authority of vesting, by law, "the appointment of such inferior officers, as they may think proper, in the President alone, in the courts of law, or in the heads of departments."

For these reasons the committee respectfully report back the bill mentioned, with a recommendation that it do not pass.

BENJ. H. HILL,
Chairman.

On the 22d September, the question being on concurring in the report of the committee, Mr. YANCEY spoke as follows;

MR. PRESIDENT: The appointment of Brigadier-Generals from a particular class, as a general rule, and the disregard shown to the claims of the States to a proper distribution of those officers among them, has induced me to offer this bill. The Judiciary committee has reported it to be unconstitutional, because it restricts the right of the President to appoint. I am informed that there are five members of that committee and that but three met, and but two favored the report. (It was here explained that while this was true, yet the two absent members endorsed the report). I have alluded to this for one purpose only, that if the report is concurred in, and it should hereafter be quoted as a precedent, it shall be understood that it received the deliberate idvestigation of but two of the five members of the committee.

I am satisfied that the report is not sound in argument; and as it involves the giving up of an important power by the legislative body, I would be untrue to that conviction if I did not attempt to sustain my convictions by such argument as I can bring to bear upon the subject. Before I sit down, however, I shall offer a substitute, proposing the bill as an amendment to the act creating the office of Brigadier-General; for in that form it will obviate some objections made against it—and I am indebted to the Senator from Louisiana [Mr. SEMMES] for the suggestion.

The Judiciary Committee offer no argument in their report. They simply assert that Congress has no legislative authority to regulate the Executive discretion in making nominations.

I join issue with that committee. What is the power of Congress over military officers? It is to be found in the power to raise armies—and in the power to make rules for the government and regulation of the land forces. That power involves the organization, the arming, the discipline, and the police of the army. In these is the power to create offices necessary to the proper government and conduct of the army. In these alone lies the power to declare there shall be Generals, major and brigadier, Colonels, Majors, Captains and Lieutenants. The power is a legislative, not an executive power, and it is delegated in the article in the Constitution declaring the powers of Congress. The power to create an office involves the power to define it—to declare the condition and terms upon which it shall exist—and without which it shall not be an office. It is a power anterior to and underlying the executive power to nominate a person to fill it. Unless the office is created, the President has no power to nominate. That power has in fact no active existence until Congress has created the office—and when the office is created, the only power of the President to nominate, its scope and extent, is to be determined by the law of Congress creating the office. It has to be exercised according to the legislative will. It is limited and defined in fact by the terms of the law, declaring what the office is, and within what scope the nominating power is to be exercised.

The nominating power is contained in but one clause in the Constitution, and that reads thus:

"He shall nominate by and with the advice and consent of the Senate, * * * Judges of the Supreme Court and all other officers of the Confederate States, whose appointments are not herein otherwise provided for, and which shall be established by law." His power of nomination then can only exist by virtue of law. It is limited by the terms of the law. The office to which he nominates only exists in and by the terms of the law. Pray tell me what limit exists upon the legislative will to define and declare the office? Will any Senator rise in his place and declare it to be incompetent in creating an office to fix as a qualification to holding it that the person nominated shall be a citizen of the Confederate States? I pause for a reply. There is none. If, then, it is within our legislative pro-

vince to say that the President shall, in making nominations,
confine them to citizens of the Confederate States, why can we
not confine him in nominating Brigadiers to command brigades
to the citizens of the State that furnishes the troops of that
brigade? The Senator from Georgia [Mr. HILL] says—and the
Senator from South Carolina [Mr. ORR] repeats it, that if Congress can confine the nomination to a State, what prevents it
from confining it to a county—to a town—and in fact to a house
in that town. There are very few things, Mr. President, that
the wit of a Philadelphia or Georgia lawyer may not ridicule,
by running it into extreme illustrations. The Cross itself has
been its subject. It is no fair mode of dealing with a question
in such a place, at least, as the Senate. The fact with which
the Senate deals is that it is proposed to fix citizenship of a
State as a qualification to command a brigade of troops raised
in that State. Is that unconstitutional? This Congress constitutionally knows nothing of counties, or towns, or houses in
a State, but it does know a State. It is built up by and rests
upon States—and it can as well fix qualification for an office to
be citizenship in a State—as to be citizenship in the Confederate
States.

It rests upon those who hold the contrary position to bring
forward some clause in the Constitution which denies it, or
some sound argument against it.

The Senator from Mississippi [Mr. PHELAN], who always
meets an argument with fairness and gravity, says that if, under
the clause to govern the army, Congress can prescribe a qualification for a nominee, what will prevent Congress, under the
16th clause of section 8, Art. I. of the Constitution, from pre-
scribing qualifications for offices in the militia, inasmuch as the
clause gives to Congress the power to govern the militia? The
question is fair and pertinent. The answer is clear, and, to my
mind, satisfactory. It is this: The 16th clause, while it gives
Congress power to provide for governing the militia when

called into the service of the Confederate States, contains a restriction upon that power in the reservation to the States of the appointment of the officers. Without this reservation, the power to govern would be the same under both clauses.

[I believe, however, that Congress, under the power to organize the militia, has the power to prescribe the qualifications for officers.]

The spirit of the Constitution also calls for this legislation. By it when the militia of the States are called into our service, their brigades, as well as their regiments, are bo be officered from the State in which the brigades are raised. Now, the Senators from Virginia have both declared that they find the only constitutional power to pass the conscript act in the power to call for the militia, and one of those Senators [Mr. HUNTER] declared that act to be a substantial, though not literal, compliance with that provision in the Constitution. To these Senators, then, this bill addresses itself with peculiar force. If that law rests on the militia clause, then it is imperative with them, and all who think with them, to vote for the bill, because it so far complies with that provision as to require State troops to be officered from the State from which they come. Although it is true that the States do not make the appointment under this bill, yet the Senator from Virginia [Mr. HUNTER] cannot make that an objection, inasmuch as he voted for the conscript act, which, in cases of vacancies, gives to the President the power to nominate, but restricts his nomination to the corps in which the vacancy occurs.

Thus much, Mr. President, for the constitutional argument. There is another view of the case, derived from precedent, which is persuasively in favor of the bill and against the positions of the committee. The constitutional power of Congress to restrict nominations by law has never before been questioned. Under the late Federal Union a law was passed creating near three hundred offices, to be filled by the appointment of cadets at West Point. The law, while creating the offices and fixing the salary, made it incumbent upon the President to appoint as many *from each State* as that State had representatives. The office of commandant was created. The law creating it declared that he should be nominated from one of four persons—either the instructor of infantry, or of cavalry, or of artillery, or of engineers. The office of annual visitors to the academy was created. The law declared that the President should select them *from one-half of the States* alternately. So much for the late Union. These laws were never questioned upon the score of unconstitutionality. Even in our brief career we have similar precedents. At the last session, after an elaborate debate in this body, the conscript act was passed. One of its provisions was, that when vacancies in regimental offices occurred, they should be filled by nomination of the President, by and with the advice and consent of the Senate.—but *he was restricted by the law to the regiment* in which the vacancy occurred. The law received the sanction of both Houses, and was approved by the President, and though the constitutionality of the act in other particulars was freely discussed, this restriction was not declared to be unconstitutional by any one. The same provision has been re-enacted and reaffirmed in provisions of the new conscript bill in both Houses at this session, and yet this restriction has not been touched upon as unconstitutional. [Mr. SEMMES said: The Senate at its last session created the office of Admiral, and restricted the President in nominating to fill it "to the grade immediately below the one to be filled." It is a case in illustration of the argument of the Senator from Alabama).

I come now, Mr. President, to the policy of legislating on the matter. The President, an educated military man, with the well known peculiar views engendered by such an education, seems to have confined his nominations for Brigadier Generals, in a very large degree, to West Pointers. That may account also for the fact that his nominations preponderate so largely from Virginia, with whose young men that institution has always been a favorite. Having an unlimited power of nomination—Congress not having indicated a will to restrict it, he has chosen to exercise it according to his own ideas of men—to which of course no one has a right to object. I have no idea that the President has designed to work an injustice to any men or any State, but in my opinion the practical working of the present system has operated that injustice—in my State a marked injustice. I understand that there are about one hundred and twenty Brigadier Generals in the army. Just before the close of the last session I called at the office of the Adjutant General, and obtained a list of the brigadiers. By it I found that Virginia had twenty-nine. (Mr. PRESTON corrected Mr. Y., and said by a corrected statement, it was ascertained that Virginia had but seventeen).

I do not desire to be considered as begrudging these honors to the sons of Virginia; I hope she will get all that is her due, but she has certainly in this matter more than her proportionate share. For instance I believe Alabama had more regiments in the Provisional Army of the Confederate States than Virginia has ever had. She has furnished, as I have been informed, sixty-five regiments of infantry, several of cavalry, several independent battalions, and about one hundred companies which have joined regiments out of the State—yet Virginia has, according to an admitted statement, seventeen Brigadier Generals, and Alabama has but four, though she was the first to arm. Tennessee, I am told, with about the same number of troops as Alabama, has only four or five Brigadier Generals—other States are similarly treated. Besides those now commissioned, as if to deepen the disparity and to originate and perpetuate State jealousy, there are now in command of brigades, with a view doubtless to nominations, six more Virginians—while out of the gallant men of Florida, Texas, Georgia, Arkansas, Tennessee,

Missouri, Mississippi, and of Alabama, but one has been selected from each State as worthy of that position. What is the cause of this? Who will rise here and assert that the real reason is that there is no military talent in these States from which to select Brigadiers? As for myself I scout the idea. As far as Alabama is concerned, the history of the war disproves it. From the first hostile movement by the troops of that State upon Pensacola, to the last great battle at Sharpsburg, there has not been a great battle fought upon this side of the Mississippi that her sons, have not, both as privates and regimental commanders, demonstrated that they possess, in a high degree, military spirit, genius and endurance. In the first great clash of arms upon the field of Manassas, her celebrated Fourth, by the testimony of the enemy's official report, broke four regiments of the foe in four different charges upon that gallant regiment. In one of the recent and most important battles before Richmond, though having a less number engaged than at least two other States, the killed and wounded of the Alabama regiments far outnumbered those from any other State. In the name of her gallant dead—her Lomax, her Bullock, her Jones, her Woodward, her Moore, her Hale, her Baine—in the name of her gallant but neglected and disparaged living, who now command her regiments, I pronounce the bare idea that her sons have not and do not furnish military genius and skill for Brigadier Generals to be a slander and an outrage upon her character.

If such an assertion could be truthfully made then would your militia and volunteer systems be a failure. But as long as the campaign in Mexico and this war shall be known in history that assertion will never be made. Sir, the history of the world furnishes no higher instances of skill, valor and endurance than have been almost daily furnished by the volunteers who compose our armies. If the war lingered apace at one time, the fault was in our commanders, not in our men. Bred in military schools, accustomed to command regulars, they had no confidence in volunteers. Partaking of the prejudices of their class the world over, they had not studied the great changes produced in the character of the American agriculturist by free institutions—and they had but little confidence in the ability of volunteers to stand fatigue and tremendous and prolonged fire of artillery and small arms. They, therefore, were over cautious, and more disposed to retreat and entrench than to advance and fight. It is said that during the most dreadful of the days on which the battles around this capital were raging, Gen. Lee was walking, with grave cast of countenance, back and forth at his position on the field; and when the murderous volleys were thundering most heavily on the ear, turned to a veteran General near him, and asked significantly, "Can they stand this?" "I think so," was the pithy and dry reply. And they did stand it as bravely and heroically as men ever stood in battle, and magnificently drove a superior and better disciplined foe before them. From that time to this, that great General, whom the country had thought too cautious, not sufficiently enterprising, has been the most enterprising and successful General on the continent, and I believe is so of the age. He doubts no longer. He knows the material he commands and they know him, and the consequence has been that he has led them beyond our borders, and, in two pitched battles, has severely chastised a greatly superior army on the soil of Maryland. The time has passed for the existence of doubts as to the great military aptitude and genius of the Southern people, and if there is truth in the constitutional presumption that the militia of the States can be efficiently commanded by State officers, there is equal truth in the presumption, upon which this bill is embraced, that troops raised by the Confederate Government from any one State can be efficiently commanded by generals chosen from that State.

The policy, if adopted, will also beget State emulation to excel each other. When Virginia troops are commanded alone by Virginians, and Alabama troops alone by Alabamians, it seems to me clear that State pride, that *esprit-du corps* which has at all times been deemed an invaluable sentiment in an army, will excite each to vie with the other in the noble and patriotic effort to see who can carry the barred banner deepest into the ranks of the foe.

There being no constitutional objection in the way, I cannot perceive a reason why this bill should not become a law.

NOTE.—Number of Brigadier Generals in the Confederate army as distributed among the several States on the 23d September, 1862:—[Official]. In Alabama, 6; Arkansas, 9; Florida, 5; Georgia, 11; Kentucky, 8; Louisiana, 10; Mississippi, 8; Tennessee. 11; Texas, 9; North Carolina, 10; South Carolina, 11; Maryland, 6; Missouri, 5; Virginia, 24.

From Alabama, L. P. Walker. has resigned. Gen. Rodes, appointed as from Alabama, is a Virginian, leaving to Alabama but four Brigadier Generals. Thos. J. Jackson, nominated from Virginia, is not included in the above list. Twenty-six Brigadier Generals, then, have been nominated from Virginia. Three Alabama brigades in Virginia are commanded by Virginians. Kentucky had but eight regiments in the field, previous to Kirby Smith's march.

THE PAY OF SOLDIERS.

In the Senate, October 6th, the bill to increase the pay of Privates in the army, and the substitute reported by the Military Committee to give five millions of dollars to the indigent families of the privates, being under consideration, Mr. YANCEY said:

Mr. President: In my opinion the substitute, if enacted into a law, would operate very unequally. It is designed as aid to the soldier; but to be applied to the support of his family. Its operation would be unequal in this—that a very large number probably a majority of privates in the army are single men, having no family in a legal sense. The substitute, then, would be increased compensation to one class of soldiers only—discriminating against another class—and is, therefore, unjust.

Again, the substitute discriminates between the poor and those who have a competency in the army. It is a proposition to furnish gratuitous aid from the Treasury to the poor families on account of services rendered by the heads of those families, while there is an equally large class rendering services in the army of equal value, whose families will receive no such aid from the Treasury. The operation, therefore, of such a law would be partial, unequal, unjust, and of an agrarian tendency If we ever plant the seeds in our legislative policy of a legal discrimination in favor of the poor against the rich, the time cannot be far distant in which the scenes of ancient history will be acted over again in our midst, and the wealth of the country will be seized upon and divided out amongst the improvident.

We have no right to discriminate between our citizens—either for or against rich or poor. In the view of the Constitution, all are equal who are citizens.

But there is a stronger reason still for my opposition to the substitute. It is unconstitutional—a direct and palpable violation of the Constitution. The Constitution, part 1st, section 8, Article I, says that "Congress shall have power to lay and collect taxes, duties, imposts and excises for revenue necessary to pay the debts, provide for the common defense, and carry on the Government of the Confederate States, *but no bounty* shall be granted from the Treasury." What is the grant of five millions of dollars from the Treasury to the families of indigent soldiers but a bounty? A bounty is a free gift, or liberality in bestowing favors. This, then, is a bounty. It is not pay for services—if it was, it would be given to the soldier direct, and to every soldier—whereas the substitute proposes to give the five millions to the "indigent families"—not for services rendered—but because they are "indigent"—not to a family of every soldier, but only to those of them that are "indigent." It is clearly then a bounty, and as clearly unconstitutional.

Again, the substitute offers no adequate provision for the support of the families of poor soldiers. If we have four hundred thousand soldiers, and half have poor families, it will give to each but twenty-five dollars.

For these reasons I shall vote against the substitute.

The original bill proposes to increase the pay of the privates and non-commissioned officers to fifteen dollars. Ought we to do this? I think that we should. When the law was passed fixing the pay of the private at eleven dollars a month, the currency was sound and prices at the usual rates as in times of peace. Now our currency, in which the soldier is paid, is greatly depreciated, and prices are inflated from two to ten fold. Considering the depreciation of the currency and the inflation of prices, the soldier receives now, in reality, not one-half the sum which the law designed he should receive. In fact, he can not now buy with eleven dollars one-fourth of the articles that he could buy with that sum one year ago.

For this reason I think it to be but bare justice to increase the soldier's pay at least 40 per cent.—say four dollars a month.

I am actuated also by another consideration. Without pretending to have come to a matured opinion, I am inclined to think, that under our Constitution, Congress can pass no pension law. If it be true, then, that we cannot pension the soldier wounded, maimed and broken down in the service of his country, it becomes a high duty to pay him well while he is in service.

It is said that this law will add twenty millions of dollars a year to our debt. Let it be so. Curtail the leaks and corruptions in other branches of the Government, but pay the brave and toil-worn soldier.

I shall vote against the substitute, ud for the bill to increase the pay of the privates.

www.ingramcontent.com/pod-product-compliance
Lightning Source LLC
Chambersburg PA
CBHW031803090426
42739CB00008B/1133